A Ramsgate Boy's memories of the Second World War

By

Denis Rose

ISBN: 978 1907369 41 4
© Denis Rose 1996

Published By
Michaels Bookshop 2011

Publisher's note

As you can see although Denis wrote this memoir in 1996 and died in 2001 it has only recently come to me for publication. World War 2 is fast slipping from living memory and I am anxious to obtain any other Thanet war memories for publication.

The picture on the back cover relates to the aeroplane that flew into Wellington Crescent and shows the damage to the front of the house there.

Another factor of interest to those reading this may be the school leaving age, I hope these notes are useful. The first school leaving age was set in 1880 at 10 years, this was raised to 11 in 1893, 12 in 1899, 14 in 1921, 15 in 1947 and 16 in 1968.

I would say from personal experience that the whole business of being able to work under the school leaving age extended up to about 1970 as there was much less regulation of casual employment.

The book "Thanet at War" mentioned at the beginning of this booklet is now out of print and costs around the £20 to £30 mark secondhand, other books of interest are:

"To a Safer Place; more memories of Kent evacuees" this covers Thanet, Canterbury And Ashford, was originally published in 2000 at £14.95 and I still have a few copies in stock at this price.

My own publications; "Dangerous Coastline 1939 – 1945", "Ramsgate August 1940" and "Midst Bands and Bombs 1946". These are available from our website michaelsbookshop.com where there is more information about them, or of course you can ring up or write to the bookshop, for more information or to order them, contact details at the back of this booklet.

Finally just to say I found this an interesting and edifying read that adds to my understanding of Ramsgate during the Second World War.

Michael Child
March MMXI

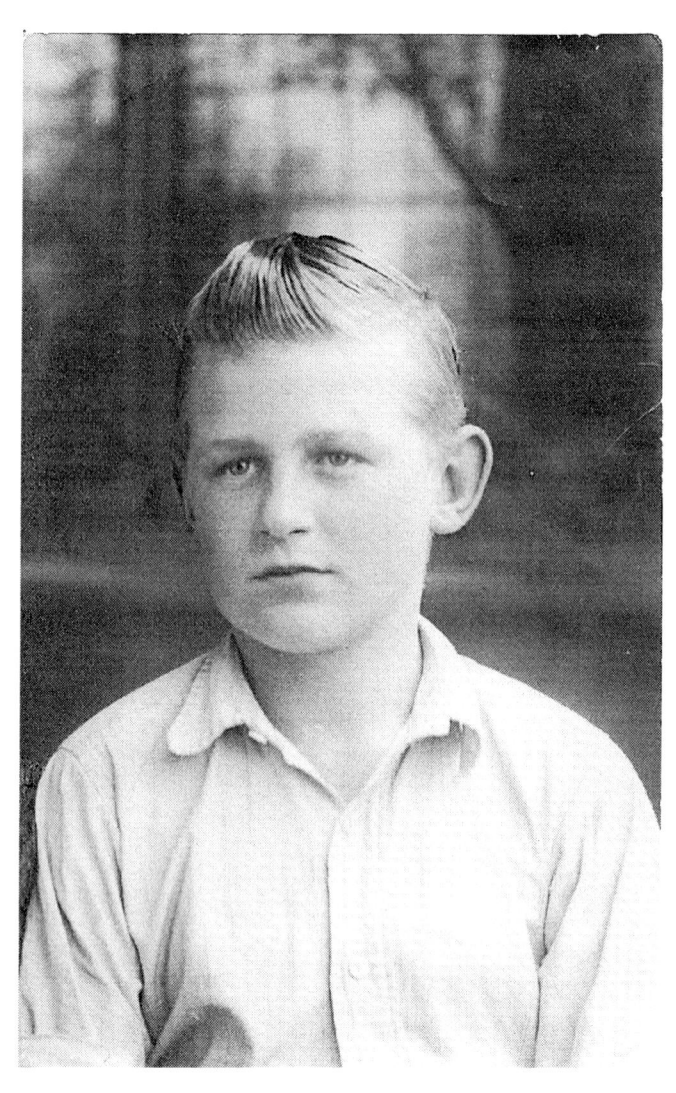

Denis Rose 15 Feb 1932 – 13 Dec 2001

ALL OF SUDDEN EVERYTHING WAS DIFFERENT

Having received a book "Thanet At War 1939 – 1945" for Xmas 1996 from my daughter and son in law, Terri and Nick, and glancing through it set me thinking back to when I was a boy.

I remember the morning the war started. It was a Sunday and everyone was going about their normal business – but all of a sudden everything was different.

A man announced on the radio that "we have had no communication from the German Chancellor, so consequently we are at war with Germany". Everything went quiet all around, out in the street and indoors, then the siren went – a long wailing sound.

My Mother said, "What do we do now?"

Nobody knew, so we got under the big wooden kitchen table. Why? I don't know. I suppose we thought it was safe there. Later the All Clear Siren went (a long continuous note) and everyone in the street went about their business.

I was seven and a half years old and that date was September 3rd 1939.

I had a sister Angela, three years younger than myself, who suffered from fits, due to a fall down the stairs when she was about two years old.

Over the next few weeks we were supplied with an Anderson Shelter, which was set up in the garden, about six feet down. We lived at 60 Winstanley Crescent.

I remember helping my father and a couple of neighbours dig out the square hole, bolt the shelter together, lower it into the hole, then cover it with dirt, stones, plants etc. This shelter was later to save our lives

DUNKIRK – "THANKS SONNY"

Life went on through the winter and spring then in May or June of 1940 we had the evacuation of Dunkirk when hundreds of wounded soldiers were brought into Ramsgate and Margate. Lots of them were taken to Ramsgate Railway Station for medical treatment at various hospitals up the line.

I went to the station to see what was going on. A woman, a first aider, grabbed me, put a pinafore around me and told me to hold it out. She then proceeded to fill it with 1^d bars of chocolate from out of the Nestle Machines in the booking hall. She told me to give them to the wounded soldiers who were lying all over the booking hall, the pavement and on the road outside the station. She said when they were all gone to come back for some more.

I passed the chocolate around and the troops were saying "Thanks Sonny - God Bless You". I went around for about an hour distributing the chocolate. Eventually all the wounded were removed by train, road etc. This all happened I think, in May or June 1940. I was eight years old now and very war experienced!

Everybody used to help everybody in those days! If you didn't all pull together you didn't survive.

AIR RAIDS – *"WE HOPED FOR THE BEST"*

The air raid warnings went off pretty regularly, night and day. Every night we had to get out of bed and either go out to the Anderson with a blanket or we got under the stairs, which housed a walk in cupboard. For some reason they thought we would be safe in there if the house was hit.

When the sirens went off during the night we had to get out of bed, dress and go to the shelter in the garden. We would be there perhaps for half an hour, an hour or more. Then the "All Clear" would go and we would go back indoors and back to bed, just get settled in bed and the siren would go again, so out of bed again, to the shelter etc as before. Sometimes this happened two or three times a night, sometimes not at all.

During the day school was restricted to a couple of hours in the morning or afternoon. If we were in class and the siren went off we would get under the desks and hope for the best.

Later they dug shelters and tunnels in the playground and we took our books, pencils etc down the tunnels with us and tried to continue our lessons.

AUGUST 24TH 1940 – "CRIES FOR HELP"

The most vivid memory I have was August 24th 1940. I was now eight and a half years old. My mother was going to make jam so sent me to get 28lbs of plums, from Solleys the greengrocers at the bottom of Victoria Hill and corner of King Street.

I went on a bike with two large shopping bags on the handlebars. I got the plums and set off home. I had just got by Boundary Road recreation ground when the Air Raid warning sounded.

I rode around by the Gas Works and the Corporation Yard, (later to become Newberrys) at the end of St. Luke's Avenue.

All of a sudden there was a terrific series of explosions. I was blown off my bike by the blast and thrown against the Corporation Yard wall. Everything went dark, just like dusk falling. There was debris, bricks, dust, and slates all flying about.

I laid against the wall covering my head with my arms. Somehow I didn't get hit with anything which was a miracle really, because the wall where I was laying was peppered with shrapnel holes yet I did't get hit.

When it began to clear I got up and started to pick up the plums which were all over the road. I put them in the bags and back on the handlebars of the bike. I WAS SCARED!

I remember the bike was all twisted, but I pushed it home because I couldn't carry the plums. Don't forget I was only eight and a half and too little.

The Gasworks had been hit; also Sussex Street, Denmark Road and the bottom of Finsbury Road had all been flattened. I had been just round the corner from all that.

The All Clear sounded as I arrived back home with the plums. I told my Mother what had happened, but she never did realize what I had been through.

I heard later that one of the gasometers had been machine-gunned and gas was escaping through a hole, which had ignited. My grandfather, who was a foreman at the gas works saved the day by blocking the hole with great hands full of clay which was used in those days to plug leaks. If the gasometer had exploded it would have taken out most of Ramsgate. My grandfather got a commendation from the King for his action that day.

About an hour later, on the same day, we were sitting on the back garden wall watching a squadron of German bombers going over when all hell broke loose.

What had happened was – there was a Boefer Gun emplacement (an anti aircraft gun) on the viaduct at Margate Road. The gun opened fired and hit the squadron leader of the bombers, straight away.

They in turn, banked around, dropped their bombs and made for home.

My Father threw us off the wall into our shelter somehow. Bombs dropped all round the Anderson that we were now in. We later found out that in all, seven bombs had dropped around us in a circle. What happened next was that the Anderson shelter was lifted out of the ground, (there was no floor to them) and all the dirt stones, rubble etc fell in on us burying us.

We were lying on the floor and under a single bed. We had been taught to NEVER SIT IN FRONT OF THE OPENING, because of the blast and shrapnel. Then the shelter came down again in its original place, thus burying us.

We, incidentally, were my father, mother, sister, myself and Mrs. Pluck and her daughter who was a friend of my mothers and was visiting.

My Grandfather came with some men from the Gas Works to get my Father to go out and repair gas mains that were leaking.

Finding us buried in the shelter they proceeded to dig us out. Luckily they arrived when they did; apparently we were buried for a few hours, and being under the bed (our heads that is), saved us from suffocating.

Afterwards I went with the men and viewed the carnage that had taken place in those few minutes of bombing.

The house was completely gutted by blast; all the inside was completely wrecked. Ceilings down, windows blown out, saucepans of jam full of plaster, half the roof gone; it was awful.

Much worse was outside. A couple of doors away, lived Mrs Finn who had a large family. Two of her children were dead and her young baby was lying alongside the chimneystack, dead. My dad got a ladder and brought the baby down – it had no arms or legs.

Opposite our back gate was the back of a house in Margate Road, where a Mrs Boxall lived. She was a nice old lady who sometimes gave us sweets or an apple. My father had helped put her Anderson in her garden. We went to see if she was alright but, unfortunately she had sat opposite the doorway, which my father had often told her not to do. A lump of shrapnel or debris had gone right through her chest and stomach. She was sitting there with her eyes open, but quite dead. If she had laid on the floor or to the side she would have been alright.

Then we heard a cry for help, but couldn't make out where it was coming from. My father finally found the source of the cry.

It was two doors down from us, the other side of our house. Aubrey Pain, who was about 18 or 20, had been blown up in the air by the blast and was wedged in a narrow gap between two pairs of houses. Incredibly he was unhurt and after some difficulty a ladder and a couple of ropes were fetched and he was rescued.

Whilst all this was taking place, the air was filled with dust and debris; it took a long time to settle. There were various people killed and injured. Bombs had landed in all different places.

My dad had a large aviary full of budgerigars. He had approximately ninety pairs of various colours, all with eggs and young at different stages.

His aviary and shed were blown apart. There were dozens of birds with legs and wings off. He had to destroy dozens of injured birds. It was a terrible shame.

The boy across the road, whom I used to play with, Roy Merrill, his Dad was killed that day. He was a lorry driver and was killed on the road away from home in his lorry.

We stayed in the house for a few days but really it was unliveable. The man from the council came to look at the damage to assess the compensation. He looked at a mattress and thought that it would be OK until my father suggested that he laid on it himself. He was persuaded to change his mind!

When we were blitzed we had no electricity or gas, so when we wanted a cup of tea or do some soup or potatoes we stood a saucepan on some bricks, or a kettle, and used a blow lamp to cook or heat water. It worked but food or water tasted of paraffin. But we were able to have a cup of tea etc. The Council found us a house in Margate Road but it wasn't long before that was bombed too.

MACHINE GUNNED – *"MY NERVES WERE SHATTERED"*

I also remember delivering newspapers with Jimmy, a boy who lived up the road. I used to go on his paper round with him. We were machine-gunned by a German fighter plane. It was by the Shakespeare Pub at the top of Chatham Street. Jimmy was killed and I never got a scratch. We were both on newsagent bikes with carriers. The bikes had bullet holes in them.

Mrs Lilley, the newsagent's wife was killed at the same time. She was standing in the shop doorway, watching us go.

I also got machine-gunned another time with my mother. It was at the top of Winstanley Crescent near the back of Darby's Garage. My mother threw me in a front garden and laid across me. Once again we were missed and very lucky.

We were on our way to the Boundary Road tunnel because we couldn't live in our house any longer. We moved down and lived in the tunnel for quite a long time whilst the Council found us another place to live. We also had a couple of rooms behind my Uncle Bert's cobbler shop in Boundary Road, which was very close to the tunnel entrance. When the warnings went we were only two minutes from the tunnel.

I also remember going to Mrs Thomas' grocery shop at the junction of Chatham Street and Park Road (the site is now occupied by a large advertisement hording) to get my mother some cigarettes. (They were eight and a half old pence for ten.)

As I was being served there was an almighty bang and Mrs Thomas grabbed me and pushed me under the counter with herself on top of me. Then we were buried under shelves of tins, jars, cartons etc. Then the ceiling came down plus a bed and wardrobe landed on top of us under the counter. We were not hurt but buried beneath tins of beans, peas, jam etc.

The shop was later demolished because it was unsafe. There were loads of shops below Mrs Thomas'. They were pulled down and the site is now occupied by Netto's car park.

Another time I was getting fish and chips for my father in Lycett's, in Chatham Street, when the siren went. Mrs Lycett took me into her dining room and put me under the table which housed a Morrison shelter. These shelters were put in houses with no gardens. I believe all of a sudden there was a terrific bang and the blast went straight through her shop, wrecking her room, but again no one was hurt. (Fish and Chips were 4 old pence)

My nerves were shattered and I was very frightened, don't forget I was only nine years old. After that last incident I went down the tunnel in Boundary Road and never came out for about six months.

LIFE IN THE TUNNELS

We had an alcove down there, it was about 8ft. x 6ft. We lived in that part and our two sets of bunk beds were opposite in the main tunnel. We had Valor stoves to cook on and lived mainly on stews and potatoes.

My mother used to put me on the top bunk above my father, which was stupid really, because, due to my bad nerves, I used to wet the bed. I remember every night getting punched out of bed from below and getting a good hiding for peeing on him. My mother never had the sense to put a rubber sheet on the bunk and I paid the price for it.

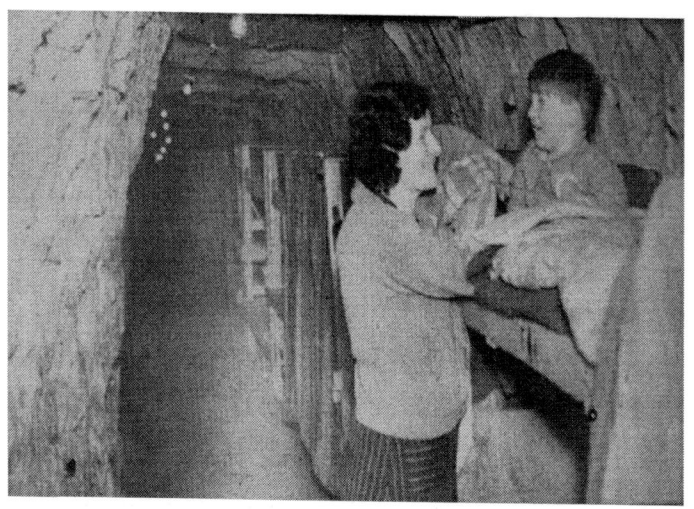

Also when lots of us had to live in the tunnels, when we were bombed out, they used to have dances down the big tunnel, this went out to the seafront where the old Ramsgate Station was situated.

They had a dance band, shops, canteen etc. Saturday was a big night and I used to walk from our alcove to the Big Tunnel (a mile or so) and watch the adults enjoying themselves. Where they held the dances they had a bar and everything. Even in the times of despair there were some highlights.

HAPPY DAYS IN DERBYSHIRE – *"RAMSARSE"*

Due to my bad nerves and getting bombed out of a further two houses provided by Ramsgate Corporation, my Grandmother Richardson had me sent to Derbyshire with some friends of hers, Mr and Mrs Dawkins. They had left Margate due to the bombing and they now lived in a little village near Ashbourne, called Mappleton.

I was to spend the happiest ten months of my life there in that cottage, it was heaven! I had never seen the countryside, a cow, a sheep etc. I had seen a horse because the milkman had one plus the coal merchant as well as the corporation carts. It was a great experience going to the country and I never ever forgot it.

I had my first Christmas presents, Christmas tree and lived with a real happy family. My own parents weren't getting on very well.

The locals used to bully me at first because to them I talked funny. They used to get me and put me in amongst the cows of which I was terrified. I had to walk to school to Ashbourne, approximately four to five miles. They used to bully me at playtime until the Headmaster put them straight and told them what I had been through. They were alright after that talk at assembly.

Life was lovely in that village. When it snowed it was about three to four feet deep. Mr Dawkins made me a sledge and at the back of the cottage was a long uphill meadow, ideal for tobogganing. It was GREAT!

The family consisted of Mr and Mrs Dawkins, Frank their son who was in the Air Force; Rene their daughter who was in the W.A.A.F.;

Pat and Daphne and Joey their son who came in the middle. Now Joey was retarded, I suppose you would nowadays say he was Spina Bifida. He couldn't control his arms and legs or talk properly. I slept in his room and after a few weeks I could understand every word he said. I used to take him out in his wheelchair, around the country lanes. He loved it! I used to help him make wool rugs. He was about twenty-three or so. I used to teach him things from my schoolbooks. We became good friends.

I should have mentioned that when it snowed we had to dig a path from the front door to the village Post Office and Stores to get food. Then a snowplough would come through and open the road to Ashbourne.

It was the happiest time of my life, that stay in that village, but unfortunately all good things come to an end.

For some reason I had to go back home to Ramsgate and the air raids.

Perhaps I should mention that sometime in the New Year Mr and Mrs Dawkins had some bad news. Their son, Frank, who was in the R.A.F. as a navigator in a bomber was shot down. They received a telegram telling them he was "missing whilst on a mission over Germany and presumed dead". There was a great sadness in that family. Then about six weeks later they were informed he was a "prisoner of war" in a Stalag camp in Poland or Germany. This brought great joy and we all had a celebration party!

We had sherry, wine and even a cake. It was lovely to see Mrs Dawkins happy again.

All the cooking, baking etc was done on a kitchen range in that cottage, no gas no electricity.

One thing I was very proud of. Mrs Dawkins took me on the bus to Ashbourne, (it ran twice a week, Wednesday and Saturday) and brought me a pair of hobnailed boots with triple studs in the soles and heels. I felt like a King. All the locals wore clogs, with wooden soles and rims round the soles and heels.

I felt wonderful, especially when they said "Gisse a look at your boots Ramsgate" That's what the village boys called me, sometimes "Ramsarse". I was so proud of them. At home I had only ever worn plimsolls'.

BACK TO RAMSGATE

My stay finally came to an end and I had to go back home to the bombing and now there was the V 1's (Doodle Bugs) I should have mentioned prior to going away, we used to stand up the top of Boundary Road and watch the 'dog fights' between the Spitfires and Hurricanes and the German fighter planes, usually Messersmitts.

One got shot down one day and the pilot bailed out and landed on the roof of the King of Denmark down Boundary Road, with his feet dangling about two feet from the ground in the alley between the Pub and the gasworks.

All the women were trying to get at him, and an amazing coincidence was that he was the spitting image of my father, blonde wavy hair and blue eyes.

My Granddad, who was a Gasworks foreman, came out of the yard and cut him down. He was a very sensible man and stopped the women from attacking him. He told them he was a prisoner of war and somebody's son who was only doing what our boys are doing the other way round. The pilot gave my grandfather his pistol and got some chocolate out of pocket for the kids. A policeman came and took him to the Police Station. He was about 18 or 19, only a lad really. He looked like a schoolboy.

His plane ended up wedged into a house on Wellington Crescent.

DOODLE-BUGS AND SHRAPNEL

We used to watch the Doodle Bugs (V1s) going over on their way to London. We also used to watch the Spitfires chasing them and then trying to shoot them down. Some pilots were that good, that after a while they used to fly alongside and touch them with their wing and turn them off course and send them back out to sea. Hundreds of these were brought down or landed on and around the South Coast.

My Father started up again breeding his budgerigars, only on a smaller scale. On a Sunday morning he used to go out on his bike to get chickweed for them. This used to grow wild in the countryside.

This particular Sunday he took me with him on the crossbar of his bike on a special little seat. We went along Pysons Road alongside the then Ramsgate Airport (which is where the Co-op Hypermarket now stands). There were no houses there, just a country lane.

We had just started picking chickweed and the warning went. All of a sudden a German fighter came over and started machine gunning along the lane. My father threw me and himself in the side of the road behind an old fallen tree trunk. Bullets were thudding into the tree trunk, but we were not hurt.

When we went to try and make it to home the bike had four bullet holes in it. Once again I had escaped injury.

But one day I wasn't so lucky. During an air raid I was running to the tunnel for shelter and got hit in the inside of my leg with what I thought was shrapnel. When it was dressed by a first aid man it turned out to be a large bolt from a bed. They were used to bolt the wooden frame and mesh spring to the bed ends. It healed alright but I still carry the scar to this day.

Amongst all this bedlam and chaos I somehow managed to pass a scholarship. I had the second highest marks and passed for Chatham House Grammar School, but couldn't go there due to my father. He said he couldn't afford it; uniform, sports gear, books etc., so I was sent to St. Georges Comprehensive, or Central. I think I still didn't get a uniform and used to have to go to school in a jumper and plimsolls, and was ridiculed by most of the teachers.

I went there at eleven and didn't have a very happy time due to my father and mother splitting up, the teachers showing me up in front of class etc.

D DAY – "THE END IN SIGHT"

The D. Day invasion in 1944 was a great memory. We all sat in the road or on walls and looked in awe, as the sky was dark with hundreds and hundreds of planes and gliders going over, taking troops to Europe for the INVASION. What a day that was; the end was in sight for the Germans!

LONDON – THE PICTURES, WORK AND MURDER

Anyway when I was twelve my father was transferred to London to work on the Gas, Light and Coke Company, as a foreman gas main layer. My mother had moved to Gillingham with my sister and was living with my Gran and Granddad. I was left with my father, a bad move on my mother's part because he took his wrath out on me most days.

Well when he was transferred to London and after a couple of months living with friends I was sent for. He had lodgings in a bedsit in Pimlico, which I had to share.

I never went to school again. While he was at work I used to fend for myself and go to the pictures at the cinema most days; it was only 6d or 9d (old money) to go in. I became quite a film buff, and today I still know all the actor's names and what films they were in and who won Oscars etc. I used to live on rice and custard, we used to have a cooked dinner on a Sunday from the landlady.

While we were living there the V2s used to come over, you couldn't hear them until they went off and they did terrible damage.

Also one night, during a raid, they dropped landmines. These used to come down in a basket on a parachute. When they touched the ground they would explode. One night a few landed on a tenement block, up the road. When we looked in the morning the tenement block of flats had completely disappeared and all that was left was a pile of rubble. There were hundreds of men, women and children killed that night! The only shelters in London apart from the Tube, were street surface shelters. These were built of brick and concrete and stood in the road and were not very safe to be in.

My father was busy in London repairing gas mains and when warnings went off I used to get in the basement of the lodgings.

On my 13th birthday my father got me a job with Carter Patersons at Aldgate, as a van guard. I was only a little tich about 4ft 10ins. It was on a horse and cart van covering Fleet Street, Blackfriars etc. delivering parcels etc. So as per my father "No more school and you can earn your living now".

The war finished and everyone celebrated V.E. Day (Victory over Europe). I was in Trafalgar Square that night and everyone went mad, jumping in the fountains, climbing the lions etc. drinks, streamers etc.

Later came V.J. Day (Victory over Japan after the atom bomb). Peace reigned again after five years. My father had met a London woman. He and my mother were now divorced. He got married and we moved back to Ramsgate.

Just before we moved back I was going to Victoria Tube Station one morning early to go to work. I had to cross a small park and discovered a soldier who had been stabbed and was dead. I got a policeman and it turned out he was a Polish soldier who had been robbed and killed.

I don't know if they found out who had done it because I never heard any more and we moved back to Ramsgate.

BACK TO RAMSGATE – WORK AND FAMILY

I got a job with a small building firm as a labourer and in 1947 after the heavy snow and big freeze I had to go and work on the bombed houses in Denmark Road. The same houses that were bombed the day I was blown off my bike with the plums.

We went to live with my Grandfather when we came back to Ramsgate and when he had my half sister, he got a council house up on Newington Estate.

He is dead now but my stepmother still lives there. I left the building firm in 1948 and got a job in Chislet Colliery as a miner. I was to work for the National Coal Board for 40 years.

Well that is my memory of the war, bombings etc. I was bombed out three times, buried twice, machine gunned four times and was lucky to come through it all. Some of my friends and their families, both in Ramsgate and London were killed and injured, so I was very lucky. I only hope future generations don't ever have to go through what we did.

I got married at 18 to a lovely girl who moved to Ramsgate in 1949 from Redditch. We had three children, two girls and a boy. They are now grown up and we have seven grandchildren. When I think back now, if I hadn't been so lucky none of them would be here today.

My wife Joy and I have just celebrated our 46th Wedding Anniversary and are still going strong. It seems incredible that it all started 58 years ago, yet it is still all vivid in my mind.

Well that's the end of my memories of the war. Please God no future generations have to go through what we did.

When it all finished and peace was restored I was still only 13 years old and had seen enough death and carnage to last a lifetime.

Denis Rose 1997

ADVERTISEMENT

When Ramsgate library burnt down and our collection of local books was destroyed I decided that the safest way to protect scarce copies of our local history books was to produce affordable reprints of them. It's now over two years since I bought the printing equipment and started work on the project.

The books fall roughly into three categories, reprints of old books about the area that have been out of print for many years – the type of thing that one would expect to find in the local archives, directories of local people and buildings – to help you to learn more about the history of your family or house and books about this area published by us for the first time – in many cases these would never be published by a commercial publisher, nor would the authors be able to afford to publish or be able to distribute them, themselves.

Printing the books as I need them means it isn't necessary to invest a large sum in any individual publication, and that I can get on with the next one straight away. One of the local authors whose book we stock had it printed himself, 800 copies cost him £12,000, the cost of the initial print run of this book i.e. 20 copies was much more manageable. I always find it surprising that the ink costs a lot more than the card and paper.

What is really nice is that when an author comes along with a book that they have written about the local area, I don't have to produce that strange sound of air rushing through the teeth that means something very expensive is going to happen, but merely tell them that they will get a 10% royalty on the selling price of the copies I print.

Michaels Bookshop,
72 King Street,
Ramsgate,
Kent
CT11 8NY

Open Monday-Saturday – 9.30 to 5.30   Closed all day Thursday

Postage to a UK address is free for our own publications.
We charge postage at cost to other countries and are happy to send books to anywhere in the world.

ORDERING ON THE INTERNET
Our website is MichaelsBookshop.com

ORDERING BY PHONE
(01843) 589500

You can telephone us between 10am and 5pm Monday – Saturday but not Thursday with your Master card or Visa number You can also leave your Master card or Visa information on our answer phone, if you do please send a confirmatory email including shipping address.

ORDERING BY POST
PAYMENT BY CHEQUE UK BANK. CHEQUES PAYABLE TO MICHAELS BOOKSHOP.

OUR PUBLICATIONS

Nr.	Title
1	The Ramsgate Tunnels Main Line Public AirRaid Shelter & Scenic Railway
2	Ramsgate in the 1900s some pictures & A Street Directory for 1900
3	Pictures of Ramsgate in the 1800s
4	Ramsgate During the Great War
5	An Assortment of the Two Discover Ramsgate Books published in 1989/90
6	A Selection of Historical Cartoons of Ramsgate
7	Broadstairs in the Early 1900s Some Pictures and a Street Directory
8	The Picturesque Pocket Companion to Margate Ramsgate & Broadstairs 1831
9	Ramsgate in the Mid 1900s a Street Directory for 1951 Some Pictures & a Map
10	A New & Complete History of the Isle of Thanet July 1828
11	Delineations Historical and Topographical of the Isle of Thanet & Cinque Ports Vol 1
12	Delineations Historical and Topographical of the Isle of Thanet & Cinque Ports Vol 2
13	1882 Catalogue Ramsgate Gunsmith
14	The History & Antiquities of the Isle of Tenet Vol. 1
15	The History & Antiquities of the Isle of Tenet Vol. 2
16	History of Birchington
17	The isle of Thanet
18	The Kentish Traveller's Companion

19	The North Foreland Lookout Post in the Great War 1915 - 1917
20	Picture of Margate and its Vicinity
21	Margate in the Early 1900s
22	The History & Antiquities of the Isle of Tenet Vol. 3
23	The Ramsgate Story
24	Thanet from the Air
25	An Isle of Thanet Directory 1849
26	Birchington & Westgate Directory 1900
27	Ramsgate Street Directory 1914-15
28	Petrified Haystack of Broadstairs
29	Margate and Ramsgate all About and Around Them a Gossiping Guide to Some Pleasant Places in the Isle of Thanet 1882
30	Picturesque Views of Ramsgate
31	Ramsgate Raids Records 1915-18
32	ZZG or the Zig Zag Guide Round and About the Beautiful Kentish Coast 1897
33	The New Ramsgate Guide 1867
34	Forty Views of Victorian Ramsgate A5
35	Forty Views of Victorian Ramsgate A4
36	Mockett's Journal
37	Historical Notes on St. Peter in Thanet 1904
38	Breezy Broadstairs
39	Happy Family of Broadstairs
40	Ramsgate and St Laurence Street Directory 1938-39
41	The War Zone In England
42	Isle of Wight
43	Midst Bands and Bombs
44	Greenwich Directory
45	Views of Late Victorian Ramsgate A5
46	Ramsgates Answer
47	Ramsgate From The Ground
48	Pictureque Excursion to Southampton
49	Historic Thanet
50	Photographs of old Ramsgate A5
51	Photographs of old Ramsgate A4
52	Views of Late Victorian Ramsgate A4

53	Picturesque Views of Ramsgate A4
54	Broadstairs Street Directory 1971
55	Ramsgate Private residents 1887
56	Ramsgate Street Directory 1887
57	The Antiquities of Richborough
58	Ramsgate & Broadstairs By camera & pen 1904-5
59	Ramsgate & Broadstairs in 1890
60	Broadstairs Street Directory 1950
61	Ramsgate Saturday August 24th 1940
62	Cockburn's Diary Ramsgate Life in the First World War
63	Weather Here Wish You were Lovely A History of Holidaying in Ramsgate
64	A Corner of Kent Ash Next Sandwich
65	A Fateful Finger of Iron (Ramsgate Pier)
66	Adventures In Shrimpville (Pegwell)
67	Broadstairs and St Peters During the Great War A4
68	Broadstairs Harbour
69	A Collection of Old Pictures of Ramsgate
70	The New Margate Ramsgate, and Broadstairs Guide 1809
71	Keble's Penny Guide to Margate and the Isle of Thanet 1885
72	A Walk in and About the City of Canterbury
73	Footpaths of Thanet
74	400 Facts and Curiosities of Ramsgate
75	The Romance of Richborough 1921
76	Thanets Raid History
77	Isle of Thanet Visitors Guide, 1901
78	Ramsgate Directory and court guide, 1878
79	Snippets of Broadstairs & St Peters
80	Broadstairs and St Peters During the Great War A5
81	3 Victorian Directories for Broadstairs and St Peters
82	Memorials of the Goodwin Sands and Their Surroundings
83	The Log of a Sky Pilot
84	An Historical Report on Ramsgate Harbour 1791
85	Storm Warriors or Lifeboat Work on The Goodwin Sands
86	A Most Strange and Curious Guide To Broadstairs
87	The Cry From The Sea and the Answer From The Shore
88	Heart of Southwood

89	A Beginner's Guide to Bathing at Broadstairs
90	From Wind To Power
91	Ramsgate Illustrated 1895
92	Come to Sunny Broadstairs Official Guide 1937
93	Twilight of the Pistons - Air Ferry - A Manston Airline
94	A Boatman's Tale
95	Childrens Convalescent Homes Of Broadstairs
96	The Mansion of Mirth - Sandgate as seen through the eyes of the Alhambra Music Hall and Rex Cinema
97	Alpha' and Better - A Modern History of St Nicholas at Wade
98	Moaning Minnie - Thanet's Civil Defence Sirens
99	All About Margate and Herne Bay
100	All About Ramsgate and Broadstairs 1864
101	Herne Bay Official Guide 1936 & Herne Bay Views Circa 1880
102	Ramsgate for 1934
103	Ramsgate - A Complete Holiday Resort
104	Birchington Great War patriotic Record
105	Occasional Ramsgate Writings
106	Ramsgate New Holiday Receipe Book
107	Kent at the Opening of the 20th Century
108	Ramsgate and Historical Thanet
109	Postcards of Ramsgate 1
110	Ramsgate All Change - Railways in the News at Ramsgate
111	Postcards of Ramsgate 2
112	Postcards of Ramsgate 3
113	Adventures in Oysterville
114	Private Residents Business Directory Ramsgate 1930
115	Westgate on Sea
116	Folkestone and it Neighbourhood
117	The History and Antiquities of the Church and parish of St Laurence Thanet in the County of Kent
118	Ramsgate Street Directory 1930
119	The Ripper In Ramsgate
120	The Hermit of Dumpton Cave
121	History of Deal
122	Private Residents Business Directory Ramsgate 1923

123	Dreamland Cinema 1935
124	Dangerous Coastline 1939-1945
125	Minster Rambles
126	The Manor of Minster and other estates.
127	Thanet Pubs
128	Lady Montifiores Cookbook
129	John Heywood's Illustrated Guide to Ramsgate
130	John Heywood's Illustrated Guide to Margate
131	Margate and Westgate with Birchington
132	Ramsgate The Kent Coast at its Best
133	Ramsgate Illustrated Photographic Views of Ramsgate, Margate and Broadstairs circa 1906
134	Pictorial Amusement Guide To Margate
135	Picturesque Excursion Down the Thames to Margate, Ramsgate and Broadstairs and their Neighbourhoods
136	Picturesque Excursion to Hastings, St. Leonards and Their Neighbourhoods 1839
137	Moaning Minnie - Thanet's Civil Defence Sirens Revised Edition
138	KT6 – An Informal History of the 6th (Thanet) Battalion of the Kent Home Guard
139	Invicta Motor Cycle Club and Biking in the Sixties
140	Ramsgate Street Directory 1923